For Dean, a really fun guy – J. K.

For my Dad – E. S.

It's lovely out,
the perfect day
for strolling down a trail.

But what's this growing on a log,
so leafless and so pale?

You crouch to look.
You're shocked to see
its cap . . . its stalk . . . its gills!

A fungus grows
among us now—
so strange it gives you chills.

Scales

Cap

Gills

Stalk

Though not a plant
or animal,
this fungus IS ALIVE!

And you can run away from it...
BUT YOU CAN NEVER HIDE.

Fungi aren't plants. They're in a group of their own that includes mushrooms, molds, and yeasts. They range from microscopic, single-celled organisms to underground systems spreading across thousands of acres. Scientists are still discovering all the fungi that exist, but the latest estimates point to between 2.2 and 3.8 million species total.

The garden seems secure and safe.
Step closer, if you dare.

Fungi can't make their own food like plants can, so they feed on living or once-living matter—like that wood mulch in your garden. And because they can't move to look for a meal, they live directly on their food source.

You'll see more mushrooms popping up.
RIGHT HERE! AND THERE! AND THERE!

Your own backyard,
so grassy green,
is full of mushrooms, too.

You can't go left...
you can't go right...
'CAUSE THEY'VE SURROUNDED YOU!

A mushroom is actually the fruit of a fungus. The rest of the fungus grows underground. As long as nothing blocks its growth, the fungus will grow in a circle around its food source, and some species of mushrooms will appear in a circle, too. Long ago, people thought mushroom rings were created by fairies, so they're called fairy circles.

Lichens aren't just fungi. Lichens are made of algae and fungi (or sometimes cyanobacteria and fungi) living together in a mutualistic relationship, which means they live better together than apart. Algae make food for the fungi to eat. Nobody is really sure what the fungi do in return, but some scientists think they help to protect the algae.

Move quickly now! Climb up this tree!
Escape the 'shrooms below.

But YIKES! That green stuff on the trunk
is fungus, too, you know.

You start to sweat.
Your heart beats fast.
There's danger everywhere.

A hundred million tiny SPORES
are blowing through the air!

Spores are tiny seed-like cells that grow into fungi. They're spread by wind, water, and even animals.

Now take a breath.

You're home at last,
those fungi left behind.

But in the darkness
of your fridge,
who knows what
you might find...

Mold is the fuzzy-looking
fungi that grow on decaying
material, like that old apple
sauce in the back of your
refrigerator.

You lock and latch the
bathroom door,
and in the dark
you cower.

But hit the lights,
and there you'll find

A FUNGUS IN YOUR SHOWER!

Mildew is a type of mold that grows in warm, damp places, like the cracks between your shower tiles.

Are you all right?
It seems your face
has turned a paler hue.

Perhaps it's not the time to share
THAT FUNGI GROW ON YOU!

Your body is a delicious buffet for many kinds of fungi. Perfectly healthy people have fungi on their skin and in their digestive systems. These fungi cause problems only when their growth gets out of hand, leading to conditions like dandruff.

But wait! Don't faint!
You'll be okay!
The chase is at its end.

These fungi aren't all horrible.
Some want to be your friends!

So don't be scared
to venture where
your dad is making lunch.

You know what's on
that pizza pie?
I bet you have a hunch...

The button mushrooms you get on your pizza are the most common edible mushrooms, but there are many other delicious kinds: shiitakes, portobellos, and oyster mushrooms, to name a few.

Did you know the most expensive food in the world is a mushroom? That's right— truffles can sell for thousands of dollars a pound!

But that's not all!
Beneath the cheese
you'll find a fun surprise.

There's *you-know-what*
in pizza dough—
yeast causes crust to rise.

Yeasts are single-celled fungi. You may not be able to see them, but they're an important ingredient in many of your favorite foods. When yeast is added to bread dough or pizza dough, it makes the dough rise and get bubbly, so the end product is light, fluffy, and delicious.

Now off you go
to toss those scraps
upon the compost pile.

With fungi's help
they'll turn to soil
(just wait a little while).

Fungi are decomposers that break down and eat dead and decaying material like fallen leaves, rotting wood, and the old food in your compost bin. This process turns that dead stuff into nutrient-rich soil that helps plants grow.

Your flowers bloom
in tidy rows.
Go on and sniff a few!

Who keeps these beds
so nice and neat?
The fungus clean-up crew.

If it weren't for fungi and other decomposers, the world would be covered in dead plants and animals. Just imagine the fall leaves piling up year after year! Fungi have been the planet's custodians for at least 400 million years, possibly longer.

It's time again
to hit the trails.
Your hike is back on track.

And look!
That chipmunk seems to like
its tasty mushroom snack.

Fungi are an important food source for many animals. Mammals, like squirrels and chipmunks, eat mushrooms, as do insects, slugs, and snails. Some species of ants, termites, and beetles even keep their own fungus farms!

Your house.
Your yard.
Your food.
Yourself.

Are fungi EVERYWHERE?

Why, yes!
THERE'S NO ESCAPING THEM...

...but aren't you glad they're there?

Meet a Mycologist

Dr. Sara Branco is a mycologist, a scientist who studies fungi at Montana State University. When she isn't busy researching in the Branco Lab, she teaches classes about fungi and microscopic creatures like bacteria. Here she is to teach you a little more about fungi!

1. Why did you decide to become a mycologist?

I fell in love with mushrooms when I was sixteen years old. I went for a hike on a fall day in a forest close to my parents' house and saw over a hundred different species of mushrooms! I had been going to that place all my life and was very surprised that I had never seen all those fungi. Where had they been hiding? That was the moment I decided I wanted to become a mycologist and understand how and where fungi live.

2. What exactly does a mycologist do?

A mycologist studies the biology of fungi. Mycologists spend their time researching how fungi grow, reproduce, and interact with their environment. This means I get to study weird places! I'm currently studying fungi that grow in soils that are contaminated with heavy metals, as well as fungi living in the hot springs of Yellowstone National Park. These springs have very hot water with a chemistry that affects the surrounding soil. My goal is to understand how fungi can tolerate these harsh conditions. Given that many fungi are very small or spend most of their life hidden, we need to use tools like microscopes and DNA techniques in order to understand them.

3. How do you study fungi?

I use a combination of field, laboratory, and computational approaches to study fungi. I go out to collect mushrooms (which is definitely the most fun part of my job!) and bring them to my lab. I work with other researchers, and together we grow fungi in Petri dishes in the lab to understand how fungi grow in nature. For example, we've been growing fungi in different conditions in our lab to understand how they tolerate the unique environments in Yellowstone National Park.

4. What's the weirdest fungus you've ever seen?

I've seen many weird mushrooms! One of the weirdest is the basket stinkhorn, a red mushroom that starts as a white egg and grows into a red lattice, forming an empty ball. It produces a foul smell of rotting flesh, attracting flies and other insects that help spread the fungus's gooey spore masses.

5. Are most fungi big or small?

They can be both! For example, baker's yeast is unicellular, meaning each individual organism is a tiny single cell. Other species form a network of cells that can grow to be really, really large. The biggest organism on the planet is actually a fungus—Armillaria gallica, also known as the humongous fungus! It covers over thirty hectares (thirty thousand square meters)! This fungus is also the oldest known organism. Scientists think it is about 2,500 years old.

6. What's one fact everyone should know about fungi?

Most people think that fungi are like plants, but they're actually more closely related to animals than anything else!

Photo Credits

Photo 1: Krisztine Gat and Annelaure Pothin

Photo 2, 3 & 4: Sara Branco

Bibliography

Bone, Eugenia. *Mycophilia: Revelations from the Weird World of Mushrooms. New York: Rodale Inc., 2011.*

Hudler, George W. *Magical Mushrooms, Mischievous Molds. Princeton: Princeton University Press, 1998.*

Marley, Greg A. *Chanterelle Dreams, Amanita Nightmares: The Love, Lore, and Mystique of Mushrooms. White River Junction, Vermont: Chelsea Green Publishing, 2010.*

Pacioni, Giovanni. *Simon & Schuster's Guide to Mushrooms. Edited by Gary Lincoff. New York: Simon & Schuster Inc., 1981.*

Rolfe, R.T. & Rolfe, F.W. *The Romance of the Fungus World. New York: Dover Publications Inc., 1974.*

Volk, Thomas. *"Fungus of the Month," Tom Volk's Fungi (website), last modified August 2010. http://botit.botany.wisc.edu/toms_fungi/fotm.html*

Library of Congress Control Number 2019930347
ISBN 9781943147649

Text copyright © 2019 by Joy Keller
Illustrations by Erica Salcedo

Illustrations copyright © 2019 The Innovation Press
Published by The Innovation Press

1001 4th Avenue, Suite 3200, Seattle, WA 98154
www.theinnovationpress.com

Printed and bound by Worzalla
Production Date March 2021

Cover lettering by Nicole LaRue
Cover art by Erica Salcedo
Book layout by Tim Martyn